LOND

UNVEILED

A Travelers Guide to the City's Hidden
Gems and Must-See Sights

Curtis O'Neill

Copyright © 2023

All rights reserved. No part of this publication may be reproduced, distributed, or transmitted in any form or by any means, including photocopying, recording, or other electronic or mechanical methods, without the prior written permission of the publisher, except in the case of brief quotations embodied in critical reviews and certain other noncommercial uses permitted by copyright law.

This guidebook is intended for personal use only and may not be resold or used for commercial purposes. The information in this book is provided as-is and the publisher assumes no liability for any inaccuracies or omissions. Readers are advised to independently verify all information before relying on it for any purpose.

TABLE OF CONTENTS

CHAPTER 1 7

GETTING TO KNOW LONDON 7

   History of London 7

   Introduction to London's Neighborhoods and Boroughs 10

   Tips for Navigating the City 13

CHAPTER 2 15

ICONIC LANDMARKS AND ATTRACTIONS 15

   Big Ben and the Houses of Parliament 15

   The Tower of London 17

   Buckingham Palace and Changing of the Guard 19

   The British Museum 22

   St. Paul's Cathedral 25

CHAPTER 3 27

HIDDEN GEMS 27

   Secret Gardens and Parks 27

   Quirky Museums and Galleries 30

- Unique markets and Shopping Districts 33
- Hidden Bars and Restaurants 36

CHAPTER 4 38

CULTURAL EXPERIENCES 38

- The West End Theatre District 38
- Classical Music and Opera Performances 41
- Contemporary Art Exhibitions 44
- London's Literary History and Bookshops 47

CHAPTER 5 49

FOOD AND DRINK 49

- Traditional British Cuisine 49
- International Cuisine in London 52
- The Best Pubs and Bars 54
- Afternoon Tea in London 56

CHAPTER 6 58

SHOPPING AND FASHION 58

- High-End Designer Boutiques 58

Vintage and Secondhand Shopping 60

Markets and Street Vendors 62

London's Fashion History and Trends 64

CHAPTER 7 67

OUTDOOR ADVENTURES 67

Parks and Green Spaces 67

Cycling and Walking Routes 69

Kayaking and Boat Tours 72

Open-Air Markets and Festivals 74

CHAPTER 8 76

FAMILY-FRIENDLY ACTIVITIES 76

Museums and Exhibitions for Kids 76

Family-Friendly Theater Performances 79

Fun Parks and Play Areas 81

Animal Encounters and Zoos 83

CHAPTER 9 85

DAY TRIPS FROM LONDON 85

Stonehenge and Salisbury 85

Oxford and Cambridge 87

Bath and The Cotswolds 90

Brighton and The Seaside 92

CHAPTER 10 94

PLANNING YOUR TRIP 94

Tips for Budget Travel 94

Accommodation Options in London 97

Hotels in London for Travelers 100

Transportation Options in London 102

Best Times to Visit London 104

CHAPTER 1

GETTING TO KNOW LONDON

History of London

One of the world's oldest and most storied cities is London. It has a lengthy, intricate past that dates back more than two millennia. The following are significant events and eras in London's history:

Roman London: The Romans established London in AD 43 as a strategic outpost on the Thames River. They gave it the name Londinium, and it quickly developed into a thriving port city and a center for trade.

Medieval London: After the Roman Empire was overthrown, London experienced a decline. It didn't start to regain its significance as a hub of commerce and a seat of power until the Middle Ages. London expanded quickly during this time, becoming one of the biggest cities in Europe.

Tudor London: London underwent significant change and upheaval during the Tudor era (1485–1603). The city witnessed the Reformation, the Tudor dynasty's ascent, and the beginning of the English Renaissance. During this time, numerous iconic structures were constructed, including the Tower of London and St. Paul's Cathedral.

The Great Fire of London: A terrible fire decimated much of the city in 1666. Over 13,000 homes, as well as numerous churches and other structures, were destroyed during the four days that the fire burned.

After the fire, London underwent a massive rebuilding effort that resulted in many of the recognizable structures and landmarks that we see today.

Victorian London: London grew to be the world's biggest and most populous city during the 19th century. It served as the nerve center of the British Empire and a major hub for international trade.

Many of London's most recognizable structures, including the Houses of Parliament and Tower Bridge, were constructed during this period.

World War II: Because the German Luftwaffe bombed London frequently, London suffered greatly during the war. The city's fortitude during the conflict and its function as a crucial ally in the struggle against Nazi Germany helped to establish its status as a major world power.

With a population of over 8 million, London is a thriving and international city that serves as a major hub for business, culture, and tourism. It is a fascinating destination for tourists from all over the world because of its numerous landmarks, museums, and historical sites, which showcase its extensive history.

Introduction to London's Neighborhoods and Boroughs

London is a city with many different and distinctive neighborhoods, each of which has its own special charm and personality. Here is a brief overview of some of London's most well-known boroughs and neighborhoods:

Westminster: The Houses of Parliament, Big Ben, and Buckingham Palace are just a few of the city's most well-known landmarks that can be found here.

Camden is a center for music, fashion, and street art and is renowned for its alternative and bohemian vibe. The renowned Camden Market can be found there, along with a thriving live music scene.

Notting Hill: This affluent area is noted for its vibrant homes, chic shops, and well-known Portobello Road Market. The Notting Hill Carnival, one of the biggest street festivals in the world, is held there every year.

Formerly a grimy industrial area, Shoreditch has recently developed into one of London's hippest districts. It has some of the best nightlife in the city, trendy bars and restaurants, and a thriving street art scene.

The Tate Modern, the Southbank Center, and the London Eye are just a few of the best cultural landmarks in London that can be found along the south bank of the River Thames.

Greenwich: This storied district is well-known for its maritime history and its lovely park, which provides breathtaking views of the city skyline. The Royal Observatory and the Cutty Sark, a legendary sailing vessel, are also located there.

Soho: This thriving area is renowned for its exciting nightlife, varied dining options, and thriving LGBTQ+ community. Many of London's theaters and live music venues are also located there.

Some of London's most prestigious and wealthy neighborhoods, such as Kensington, Chelsea, and Knightsbridge, are located in the neighboring boroughs of Kensington and Chelsea. They are renowned for their high-end shopping, stunning architecture, and top-notch museums, including the Natural History Museum and the Victoria and Albert Museum.

These are only a few of the numerous boroughs and neighborhoods that make up the interesting and diverse city of London. Each one has its own distinctive mix of entertainment, history, and culture, making it a city that never stops surprising and enthralling visitors.

Tips for Navigating the City

It can be challenging to get around in a city as big and complicated as London, especially for first-timers. Here are some pointers to get around the city:

Get an Oyster card: The easiest way to pay for public transportation in London is with an Oyster card. It can be loaded with credit and used to make bus, train, and Tube purchases. And it costs less than purchasing individual tickets.

Use a map app: Google Maps, Citymapper, and Waze are just a few of the many map apps you can use to find your way around the city. These apps can help you find the quickest routes and stay ahead of traffic.

Prior to beginning your journey, it is a good idea to plan your route and check for any unforeseen delays or disruptions. You can plan your trip using the real-time travel information on the Transport for London website.

When you can, take the time to walk around London. Many of the city's most well-known attractions are close to one another. The city's neighborhoods can be explored on foot to find undiscovered gems.

Take a double-take: If you're not used to it, driving in London requires you to adjust to using the left-hand side of the road. Never forget to always look both ways before crossing the street.

Consider taking a guided tour if you want to learn more about the city or if you're feeling overwhelmed. There are numerous different tour options, including walking, bus, and boat tours.

Never hesitate to seek assistance: If you're lost or need directions, don't be afraid to ask someone for assistance because Londoners are generally cordial and helpful.

You can easily navigate the city and make the most of your time in London by using the advice in this article.

CHAPTER 2

ICONIC LANDMARKS AND ATTRACTIONS

Big Ben and the Houses of Parliament

Two of London's most recognizable landmarks are Big Ben and the Houses of Parliament. Here is a synopsis of their background and importance:

The Palace of Westminster, also known as The Houses of Parliament, is where the British government is located. It was a royal palace when it was constructed in the 11th century.

The palace was rebuilt in the 19th century after a fire severely damaged much of the original construction. Both the House of Commons and the House of Lords are currently housed within the Houses of Parliament.

The clock tower at the north end of the Houses of Parliament is known by the moniker "Big Ben." When the tower was finished in 1859, its clock gained notoriety for being dependable and accurate. In honor of Sir Benjamin Hall, who oversaw the bell's installation and weighed more than 13 tons, the bell inside the tower was also given the nickname Big Ben.

Big Ben and the Houses of Parliament represent British democracy and government as a whole. They have also gained popularity as a tourist destination, attracting thousands of visitors annually who come to admire the stunning architecture and discover the background and workings of the British government.

A guided tour of the building is available if you're interested in learning more about the Houses of Parliament and Big Ben. This tour includes stops at the House of Commons and House of Lords as well as the chance to climb the clock tower and get a close-up view of Big Ben.

The Tower of London

One of London's most well-known historical sites, the Tower of London has contributed significantly to the city's history for more than 900 years. Here are some details and noteworthy events relating to the Tower of London:

William the Conqueror initially constructed the Tower in 1078 as a fortress to defend his new kingdom from invasion. It eventually evolved into a royal palace, a prison, and an execution site.

The history of The Tower is both fascinating and occasionally horrifying. Anne Boleyn, Sir Walter Raleigh, and Guy Fawkes were among the most well-known inmates at the Tower.

The Tower is where the Crown Jewels of England are kept, and the Jewel House is where visitors can view them on display. Some of the most priceless and renowned jewels in the entire world are included in the collection, including the Koh-i-Noor diamond and the Imperial State Crown.

The Yeoman Warders, also referred to as the Beefeaters, reside in the Tower. Since the fifteenth century, these guards have served as a constant at the Tower, giving tours and keeping the structure safe.

The renowned ravens that reside on the property are also visible to visitors to the Tower. According to legend, the kingdom will crumble if the ravens ever leave the Tower.

There are numerous tours and exhibitions available daily to visitors of the Tower. The White Tower, the Medieval Palace, and the Bloody Tower are among the attractions.

For history buffs and anyone interested in London's rich history, a trip to the Tower of London is a must. It is not surprising that the Tower is still one of the city's most popular attractions given its intriguing past and magnificent architecture.

Buckingham Palace and Changing of the Guard

The official residence of the British monarch in London is Buckingham Palace, one of the most recognizable buildings in the area. The following information about Buckingham Palace and the Changing of the Guard ceremony is provided:

The Duke of Buckingham originally had Buckingham Palace constructed in 1703 as a townhouse. King George III bought it in 1761 to use as the royal family's private residence.

The palace is surrounded by lovely gardens and parks and is situated in the center of London. Throughout the summer, the palace is open to visitors who can tour the State Rooms and view some of the royal collection on display.

The ceremony known as "Changing of the Guard" is held in front of Buckingham Palace every day. One regiment replaces another during the ceremony's changing of the guard in a show of military precision and pageantry.

The ceremony occurs every day in the summer and every other day in the winter. It's a well-liked attraction for tourists in London, and lines frequently form early to get a good view of the action.

The Old Guard arrive first and are examined by the New Guard before the ceremony can begin. The Old Guard leaves the palace and is replaced by the New Guard after they march together to the music of a military band.

Visitors have the opportunity to witness a custom that has been practiced at Buckingham Palace for more than 350 years during the Changing of the Guard, which is a singular and unforgettable experience.

Be sure to put Buckingham Palace and the Changing of the Guard on your itinerary if you're going to be in London. It's an opportunity to get up close and personal with a piece of British history and pageantry.

The British Museum

Some of the most impressive collections of human history and culture can be found at the British Museum, one of the most well-known and frequently visited museums in the world. Here are some details and noteworthy events related to the British Museum:

The first national public museum in the world, the British Museum opened its doors in 1753. Over the years, its collection has expanded, and it now contains over 8 million items from various cultures and historical eras.

The Elgin Marbles, the Sutton Hoo treasure, and the Rosetta Stone are a few of the most well-known and expensive items in the museum's collection. These items not only have great aesthetic appeal and financial value, but also significant historical and cultural value.

With displays on Ancient Egypt, Greece and Rome, the Middle East, Asia, Africa, and the Americas, the museum's galleries are arranged by continent and theme. Additionally, there are galleries devoted to particular subjects like coins, medals, prints, and drawings.

The building itself is an impressive neoclassical structure created by architect Sir Robert Smirke, which is another noteworthy aspect of the museum's architecture. A number of eateries and shops can be found inside the renowned Great Court, which has a glass roof and is a well-known tourist destination in and of itself.

The British Museum is open to the public without admission charge, but some special exhibitions might. For visitors who want to learn more about the museum's collections, there are a variety of guided tours and talks available.

Anyone who enjoys history, culture, or art ought to visit the British Museum. It is understandable why the museum continues to rank among London's top attractions given its extensive collections and stunning architecture.

St. Paul's Cathedral

One of London's most well-known and recognizable landmarks, St. Paul's Cathedral is a must-see for anyone with a passion for the past, modern architecture, or religion. Here are some details and noteworthy features of St. Paul's Cathedral:

The St. Paul's Cathedral, which is in the center of London's financial district, is a significant representation of the city's tenacity and resiliency. The Great Fire of London and World War II are two of the city's most important historical occurrences that the cathedral has endured.

Sir Christopher Wren, one of the most renowned architects in British history, created the current cathedral between 1675 and 1710. One of the largest domes in the world, the cathedral's dome is a testament to Wren's engineering and design prowess.

The ornate High Altar, the intricate choir stalls, and the lovely mosaics on the interior of the dome are just a few of the impressive artworks and monuments that can be found at St. Paul's Cathedral. Some of

Britain's most well-known historical figures, including Lord Admiral Nelson and Sir Winston Churchill, also have tombs in the cathedral.

The history, architecture, and artwork of St. Paul's Cathedral can all be learned more about by taking guided tours. They can also ascend to the dome's summit to take in breath-taking panoramas of London's skyline.

Daily services are held every day of the week at the cathedral, which is still a functioning house of worship. Visitors are welcome to participate in these services or just spend some time alone in the serene surroundings of the cathedral.

In addition to providing visitors with a chance to engage with London's rich history and culture, visiting St. Paul's Cathedral is a singular and unforgettable experience. No matter if you have an interest in architecture, the arts, or religion, St. Paul's Cathedral is a must-visit site.

CHAPTER 3

HIDDEN GEMS

Secret Gardens and Parks

While many of London's parks and gardens are well-known and frequently crowded, there are also many undiscovered gems tucked away all over the city. Here are some hidden parks and gardens in London that are worth visiting:

Kyoto Garden is a quiet Japanese-style garden tucked away in Holland Park that provides a tranquil escape from the hustle and bustle of the city. The garden is a well-liked location for picnics and photography because it has a pond, a waterfall, and stunning cherry trees.

Postman's Park is a peaceful haven in the midst of the city and is situated close to St. Paul's Cathedral. A moving memorial to everyday heroes, including those who lost their lives trying to save others, can be found in the park.

The park is a tranquil place where visitors can stroll while considering the courage and sacrifice of these people.

The Horniman Museum Gardens are a hidden gem that provide breathtaking views of the city and are situated in the south-east of London. The gardens include a lovely rose garden, a natural history trail, and a Victorian conservatory. The museum's eclectic collection of artifacts, which includes taxidermied animals and musical instruments from all over the world, is another attraction for visitors.

Red Cross Garden: The Red Cross Garden is a tranquil green area tucked away in Southwark that was first created as a model garden for nearby residents in the late 1800s. The garden has a lovely pond, seating areas, and a monument honoring those who lost their lives in a tragic factory fire that happened nearby in 1911.

Nomadic Community Gardens: The Nomadic Community Gardens are an energetic and diverse green space in Shoreditch that honors art, culture, and community. Along with a community cafe and event space, the gardens include sculptures, a variety of plants and flowers, and vibrant murals.

Visitors have the opportunity to find some of the city's hidden gems while escaping the crowds in London's secret gardens and parks. These hidden gems are definitely worth exploring, whether you're looking for a peaceful retreat or a bustling community space.

Quirky Museums and Galleries

There are numerous oddball museums and galleries in London that provide a glimpse into unusual subjects and themes. Here are a few of London's most intriguing and unusual museums and galleries to visit:

The Viktor Wynd Museum of Curiosities is a tiny, oddball museum in Hackney that is full of strange and fascinating items, like a lamb with two heads and shrunken heads. The museum has a bar where guests can enjoy cocktails while being surrounded by oddities.

The Sir John Soane's Museum is located in the former residence of Sir John Soane, an architect who amassed a significant collection of artwork, artifacts, and oddities over the course of his lifetime. There are many unusual items in the museum, including Hogarth paintings, Egyptian sarcophagi, and even Napoleon's toothbrush.

The House of Illustration is a gallery in King's Cross that exhibits the work of illustrators from all over the world, from political cartoons to illustrations for children's books. Additionally, the gallery hosts discussions, workshops, and events centered around design and illustration.

The Cartoon Museum in Bloomsbury features exhibits that feature well-known cartoon and comic book characters like Dennis the Menace and Desperate Dan. For aspiring cartoonists and animators, the museum also hosts events and workshops.

The Grant Museum of Zoology is a museum with an impressive collection of animal specimens, including a dodo skeleton and a jar of moles. It is located at University College London. A giant squid and a collection of preserved brains are also on display at the museum.

The Museum of Brands is a quirky museum in Notting Hill that features displays of vintage goods and packaging from the 1800s to the present day.

It explores the history of consumer culture and advertising. Visitors can learn about how products like Coca-Cola and Cadbury's chocolate have changed over time and even sample some traditional treats in the museum cafe.

A unique and unconventional way to learn about the history and culture of the city is through London's quirky museums and galleries. These museums and galleries will astonish and delight you whether you have an interest in strange objects, unusual art, or offbeat subjects.

Unique markets and Shopping Districts

There are many different places to shop in London, from upscale department stores to unique independent boutiques. The following London shopping areas and markets are worth checking out:

Camden Market is a vast network of markets that sells everything from vintage clothing to street food. It is situated in the bustling Camden Town neighborhood. A bite to eat from one of the many food vendors or a stroll through the stalls selling handmade jewelry, original home décor, and alternative clothing are both options open to visitors.

Portobello Road Market: This well-known street market in Notting Hill is distinguished by its vibrant structures and eclectic assortment of antiques, vintage apparel, and knickknacks. Along the bustling street, visitors can also find locally grown food, handcrafted goods, and street performers.

Brick Lane Market is a diverse collection of markets that sell everything from handmade jewelry to vintage clothing. It is situated in the hip East End neighborhood. Additionally, visitors can sample mouthwatering street food from various countries, such as Middle Eastern specialties, Indian curries, and traditional British fare.

Covent Garden: This prestigious shopping area in the center of London is renowned for its exquisite architecture. Visitors can shop for designer apparel and accessories, artisanal cosmetics, and one-of-a-kind gifts, watch a street performance, and eat in the crowded piazza.

Borough Market is a bustling food market close to London Bridge that offers artisanal cheeses, meats, and fresh produce at its many stalls. Additionally, tourists can purchase and sample regional craft beer and wine as well as international treats like Spanish paella and French pastries.

Columbia Road Flower Market: With its vibrant blooms and fragrant plants lining the street, this thriving flower market in the East End is a feast for the senses. Along with a wide selection of flowers and plants, the market offers handmade crafts and garden accessories.

London's distinctive markets and shopping areas provide an opportunity to find one-of-a-kind items, savor delectable cuisine, and become immersed in the city's vibrant culture. These markets and areas are sure to satisfy your urge to shop, whether you're looking for vintage clothing, fresh produce, or unique souvenirs.

Hidden Bars and Restaurants

There are many hidden bars and restaurants that provide a distinctive and intimate experience in London, which is renowned for its thriving nightlife and culinary scene. Here are some of London's best secret bars and eateries:

Nightjar is a speakeasy-style bar with a glitzy and cozy ambiance that is situated in the hip East End neighborhood. The bar features live entertainment and craft cocktails that are inspired by the jazz era.

Cahoots: This Soho underground bar features retro furnishings and specialty drinks that are designed to resemble an abandoned tube station from the 1940s. With swing dancing events and live music, the bar provides a fun and engaging experience.

Evans & Peel Detective Agency: This eccentric bar in Earl's Court has a hidden entrance and a detective-themed cocktail menu that is designed to resemble a private detective agency from the 1920s. To enter the bar, guests must make a reservation and supply a password.

Gordon's Wine Bar is a venerable establishment that has been serving wine and cheese since 1890. It is situated in an underground cellar not far from Embankment. With tables lit by candles and a large selection of wines and sherries, the bar has a warm, rustic atmosphere.

The Culpeper is a secret rooftop bar in Shoreditch that has beautiful views of the city skyline as well as a garden and greenhouse that supply the bar's food and cocktail menu with fresh herbs and vegetables.

The Mayor of Scaredy Cat Town is an eccentric bar in Spitalfields that is concealed behind a refrigerator door in a well-known breakfast establishment. The bar offers inventive cocktails and a fun atmosphere, but guests must ask to see "the mayor" in order to enter.

Escape the crowds and find one-of-a-kind, unforgettable experiences at London's hidden bars and restaurants. These hidden gems are sure to please, whether you're in the mood for a cozy wine cellar, a hidden speakeasy, or a themed bar.

CHAPTER 4

CULTURAL EXPERIENCES

The West End Theatre District

The West End Theatre District is a center of culture in London and is renowned for its wide variety of theatrical productions, including both traditional plays and modern musicals. Here are some of the West End Theatre District's highlights:

The National Theatre is a renowned organization that presents a wide range of productions, including Shakespeare as well as contemporary plays and experimental pieces. It is situated on the South Bank of the River Thames. The structure itself is a work of modernist architecture that provides breathtaking views of the river.

The Royal Opera House, which is housed in Covent Garden and hosts both the Royal Ballet and the Royal Opera, presents a range of productions, from traditional operas to modern dance performances.

The structure is beautifully designed in the Neoclassical style, with elaborate interiors and a large auditorium.

The West End Musicals: The West End is renowned for its thriving musical theater scene, which features productions ranging from time-honored favorites like Les Miserables and The Phantom of the Opera to fresh and avant-garde works like Dear Evan Hansen and Hamilton.

A number of renowned theaters, including the London Palladium and the Theatre Royal Drury Lane, can be found in the West End.

Shakespeare's plays were originally performed at the Elizabethan playhouse known as The Globe Theatre, which is situated on the South Bank of the River Thames. Shakespearean plays of all kinds are presented at the theater, along with fresh productions and live musical performances.

The Harold Pinter Theatre is a venerable theater in the center of the West End that bears the name of the British playwright and actor.

The theater features a variety of productions, including new plays by up-and-coming playwrights as well as classic plays.

The English National Opera is housed at the London Coliseum, an opulent Edwardian theater close to Trafalgar Square. The theater presents numerous operatic productions, in addition to ballet and modern dance performances.

The West End Theatre District provides a variety of theatrical experiences, including both traditional plays and cutting-edge contemporary productions. Shakespearean plays, musicals, and operas are all available in the West End, so whatever your tastes, you're sure to find something there.

Classical Music and Opera Performances

With a vibrant and diverse cultural scene, London is home to some of the best classical music and opera venues in the world. Here are some of London's best opera and classical music performances:

The Royal Albert Hall is a renowned venue in South Kensington that hosts a wide range of classical music and opera performances as well as pop and rock concerts. It is renowned for its stunning circular design and world-class acoustics. Every summer, the location also plays host to the BBC Proms, a series of concerts that honors classical music and features some of the best orchestras and soloists in the world.

The Royal Opera House, which houses both the Royal Opera and the Royal Ballet, is located in Covent Garden and presents a range of productions, including new and experimental pieces as well as well-known operas like La Boheme and Don Giovanni. Backstage tours and educational programs are also provided by the venue.

The Barbican Centre is a renowned performing arts center in the City of London that presents a range of classical music and opera performances in addition to theatre, dance, and visual arts. A variety of concerts and events are held at the location throughout the year. It is the home of the London Symphony Orchestra and the BBC Symphony Orchestra.

Wigmore Hall: Located in the heart of London's West End, Wigmore Hall is a historic concert venue renowned for its enchanting acoustics and cozy atmosphere. Some of the best classical musicians and singers in the world perform at the venue, which hosts a variety of chamber music and song recitals.

St. Martin-in-the-Fields: Located in Trafalgar Square, St. Martin-in-the-Fields is a historic church that regularly hosts choral and chamber music performances. The location also provides a variety of educational programs and neighborhood outreach projects.

English National Opera: The English National Opera is a renowned opera company that presents a range of productions at the London Coliseum, including new and experimental works as well as well-known operas like Tosca and The Marriage of Figaro. Additionally, the business has outreach programs and educational initiatives.

With venues and performances that feature some of the best musicians and singers in the world, London's classical music and opera scene offers a rich and diverse cultural experience. Whatever your tastes, London is sure to have something to offer, whether you're in the mood for a chamber music recital or a classic opera.

Contemporary Art Exhibitions

A variety of galleries and museums in London feature the most recent creations from both established and up-and-coming artists. The city is home to a thriving contemporary art scene. The following are some of the highlights of London's current art exhibitions:

On the South Bank of the River Thames, in a former power plant, is the Tate Modern, one of the most renowned museums of modern art in the world. The museum houses a variety of contemporary art exhibitions and installations in addition to a global collection of modern art.

Saatchi Gallery: Located in Chelsea, the Saatchi Gallery is a museum of contemporary art that features the most recent creations by internationally renowned and up-and-coming artists. A variety of exhibitions and installations, including painting, sculpture, photography, and video art, are on display at the gallery.

The Serpentine Galleries are two modern art galleries that are situated in Kensington Gardens. The galleries offer a schedule of talks and events in addition to a variety of exhibitions and installations by contemporary artists.

Whitechapel Gallery: Located in the heart of East London, the Whitechapel Gallery is a contemporary art museum that features the newest creations from both up-and-coming and renowned artists. The gallery offers a variety of exhibitions and installations in addition to a schedule of events and talks.

Hayward Gallery: Known for its avant-garde and experimental exhibitions, the Hayward Gallery is a contemporary art museum on the South Bank of the River Thames.

Contemporary works of art in the gallery range from painting and sculpture to installations and video art.

The Institute of Contemporary Arts (ICA) is a modern art museum with a location in The Mall and a reputation for hosting cutting-edge events and exhibitions. The museum showcases a variety of contemporary art, including digital media, painting, and sculpture.

The contemporary art scene in London features a wide variety of exhibitions and installations by both up-and-coming and well-established artists, showcasing the most recent developments in the art world. Whether you enjoy sculpture, installation, painting, or video art, London is sure to have something to inspire and enthrall you.

London's Literary History and Bookshops

From the writings of Shakespeare and Dickens to contemporary authors like J.K. Rowling and Zadie Smith, London has a rich literary history. Here are some of London's literary history's and bookshops' highlights:

Visit Shakespeare's Globe, a replica of the Southwark theater where the Bard's plays were presented in the 16th and 17th centuries. To find out more about the past of this renowned theater, go to a performance or a tour led by an expert.

Discover one of London's most well-known authors' life and works at the Charles Dickens Museum in Bloomsbury. Dickens-related artifacts and exhibits can be found at the museum, which is housed in the home where he lived from 1837 to 1839.

The British Library is the country's national library and is home to more than 150 million items, including books, manuscripts, maps, and other items.

View original drafts of works by well-known authors like Virginia Woolf and Jane Austen, or go to the ongoing display "Treasures of the British Library."

Bookstores: London is home to a large number of independent bookshops, each with a distinct personality and allure. Visit Persephone Books in Bloomsbury, which specializes in publishing lost works by female authors, or Daunt Books in Marylebone, which is renowned for its Edwardian architecture and extensive travel section. Hatchards in Piccadilly, Foyles in Charing Cross Road, and Waterstones in Gower Street are a few additional notable bookstores.

Literary walking tours: Take a narrated walking tour to learn more about London's literary past. Explore the locations that influenced Virginia Woolf in Bloomsbury, follow in the footsteps of Sherlock Holmes and Dr. Watson on Baker Street, or see the locations of Charles Dickens' residence and workplace.

CHAPTER 5

FOOD AND DRINK

Traditional British Cuisine

With influences from Roman, Anglo-Saxon, Viking, and Norman cuisines, traditional British cuisine is a reflection of the history and culture of the nation. Check out these traditional British dishes:

The traditional British dish known as "Fish and Chips" consists of battered and deep-fried fish, typically cod or haddock, along with chips (thick-cut French fries) and a side of mushy peas. It is a mainstay of British cooking and is available in all fish and chip shops across the nation.

Roast on Sunday: A Sunday roasts are a traditional British meal that typically include roast beef, lamb, or pork as well as roasted vegetables, potatoes, and gravy. Yorkshire pudding, a savory baked pudding made with flour, eggs, and milk, is frequently served with it.

Bangers and Mash: Also known as bangers and mashed potatoes, this hearty dish is frequently served with gravy and peas. It's a well-liked comfort food that can be found in eateries and pubs across the nation.

A traditional British dish known as shepherd's pie is made with ground beef or lamb, mashed potatoes, and vegetables like carrots, onions, and peas. It's a warming and hearty dish that's ideal for a chilly winter day.

Steak and Kidney Pie: Made with diced beef and kidneys, as well as vegetables like onions and carrots, Steak and Kidney Pie is a savory pie baked in a pastry crust. It is a typical British dish that is frequently offered in pubs.

Black Pudding is a type of sausage made from oatmeal, oatmeal fat, and blood from pigs. It is a typical British dish that is frequently included in a full English breakfast.

Eton Mess: Made of whipped cream, crumbled meringue, and strawberries, Eton Mess is a traditional British dessert. It's a straightforward dessert that tastes great and is ideal for summer.

These are merely a few illustrations of typical British dishes. With many regional specialties and unusual ingredients, British cuisine has a long and interesting history. There is a British dish that you will enjoy whether you enjoy hearty meat dishes or sweet desserts.

International Cuisine in London

Because London is a melting pot of cultures, you can find a wide variety of international cuisine there. Here are a few instances:

Indian: Since there is a sizable Indian community in London, there are a ton of excellent Indian restaurants to choose from. The Brick Lane district of East London is home to some of London's top Indian eateries.

Chinese: Since there are many Chinese people living in London, there are a lot of great Chinese restaurants to choose from. The West End's Chinatown is a great location to find real Chinese food.

Italian: There are many excellent Italian restaurants in London that serve everything from traditional pizza to fresh pasta dishes. For Italian food, Soho and Covent Garden are particularly excellent neighborhoods.

Middle Eastern: Lebanese, Turkish, and Persian cuisine are all served in a variety of restaurants throughout London's thriving Middle Eastern food scene. The Edgware Road neighborhood is home to some of London's top Middle Eastern eateries.

Japanese: Over the past few years, many top-notch sushi and ramen restaurants have popped up all over London, fueling the city's growing interest in Japanese cuisine. The best places to eat Japanese food are in Soho and Covent Garden.

Mexican: The Mexican food scene in London is expanding, and many restaurants offer real Mexican food. For Mexican food, Dalston and Shoreditch are particularly excellent neighborhoods.

These are merely a few illustrations of the numerous varieties of international cuisine available in London. In this multicultural city, you can find something delicious no matter what your taste.

The Best Pubs and Bars

With numerous storied pubs and contemporary bars spread out across the city, London has a thriving pub scene. The following are a few of the top bars and pubs to visit:

The Churchill Arms is a renowned pub in Notting Hill that is renowned for both its charming interior and lovely floral exterior. It offers a wide variety of beers and classic pub fare.

The Ye Olde Cheshire Cheese in the City of London is a historic pub that dates back to the 17th century. It has a number of quaint nooks and crannies where patrons can relax with a drink. It offers a wide variety of beers and traditional pub fare.

The Princess Louise is a magnificent Victorian pub in Holborn that is renowned for its opulent decor and wide variety of beers. It's a well-liked location for drinks after work.

The Sky Garden: This City of London rooftop bar offers breathtaking views of the city skyline. It offers a selection of cocktails, wine, beer, and small plates.

The Old Vic, a famous theater in Waterloo, has a great bar and cafe area that's ideal for pre- or post-show beverages. It offers a wide variety of small plates, wines, and beers.

The Gibson is a chic cocktail lounge in Clerkenwell that is well-known for its inventive and delectable concoctions. Both the ambiance and the selection of spirits are excellent.

The Ten Bells: This Spitalfields landmark bar, which dates to the 18th century, is well-known for its connection to Jack the Ripper. It offers a wide variety of beers and classic pub fare.

The Blind Pig in Soho offers a wide variety of inventive cocktails in a speakeasy-style setting. It has a warm atmosphere and is ideal for a special occasion or date night.

Afternoon Tea in London

There are many fantastic locations in London to take afternoon tea, which is a classic British tradition. Some of the top locations for afternoon tea are listed below:

The Ritz is a well-known hotel in Piccadilly that is famous for its opulent afternoon tea, which features scones with clotted cream and jam, pastries, and a variety of sandwiches. It is offered in the magnificent Palm Court of the hotel.

Another venerable Mayfair hotel, Claridge's serves traditional afternoon tea with a contemporary twist. Along with a variety of tea blends, it offers a selection of finger sandwiches, pastries, and scones.

Sketch: This chic Mayfair eatery is renowned for its eccentric design and creative flair. The Gallery, a pink-hued space with whimsical art and furnishings, serves afternoon tea.

The Wolseley: This opulent Mayfair cafe-restaurant is renowned for its traditional European fare and opulent ambiance. The magnificent dining room, which has high ceilings and Art Deco-inspired furnishings, serves afternoon tea.

A variety of sandwiches, pastries, and scones are served at the elegant afternoon tea served at the Savoy, a famous hotel on the Strand. It is provided in the stunning glass dome-topped Thames Foyer of the hotel.

For its premium teas and other gourmet foods, Fortnum & Mason is a venerable department store in Piccadilly. The store's Diamond Jubilee Tea Salon, which has an opulent atmosphere and an excellent selection of teas and pastries, serves afternoon tea.

These are just a few of the many wonderful locations in London where you can take afternoon tea. You're sure to find something to suit your tastes in this city, whether you're searching for a traditional tea experience or something more contemporary.

CHAPTER 6

SHOPPING AND FASHION

High-End Designer Boutiques

London is a top location for high-end designer shopping, and the city is dotted with upscale boutiques and department stores. Here are some of London's top locations for shopping high-end clothing:

A wide variety of upscale shops can be found on Mayfair's Bond Street, including the flagship locations of Louis Vuitton, Chanel, and Burberry.

The renowned Knightsbridge department store Harrods is renowned for its extensive collection of high-end fashion brands, as well as its opulent interiors and impressive food hall.

Selfridges: Selfridges, a renowned department store on Oxford Street, carries a number of high-end fashion labels, such as Gucci, Prada, and Balenciaga.

Sloane Street in Knightsbridge is well-known for its abundance of upscale shops, including outlets for labels like Dior, Tom Ford, and Cartier.

Several upscale clothing boutiques, including ones for Celine, Roksanda, and Christopher Kane, can be found on Mayfair's Mount Street.

Dover Street Market is a cutting-edge concept store in Mayfair that is renowned for its avant-garde approach to retail and cutting-edge fashion brands.

There are countless high-end designer boutiques and department stores in London; these are just a few examples. In this fashion-forward city, you can find anything you're looking for, from cutting-edge fashion to traditional luxury shopping.

Vintage and Secondhand Shopping

With a wide selection of markets, boutiques, and secondhand stores dispersed throughout the city, London is a great place to shop for vintage and secondhand clothing and accessories. Some of London's top stores for secondhand and vintage clothing are listed below:

East London's Brick Lane Market is renowned for its eclectic selection of vintage home goods, clothing, and accessories. In the area, there are a lot of secondhand shops and vintage boutiques.

Beyond Retro: One of London's biggest and most well-known vintage shops, with locations in Soho and Dalston. They provide a broad selection of vintage apparel, accessories, and footwear dating from the 1920s to the 1990s.

Rokit: Another well-known vintage retailer with several locations in London, Rokit sells a carefully curated assortment of retro apparel and accessories in addition to its own line of retro items that have been upcycled and altered.

Oxfam: This well-known chain of charity shops has locations all over London and provides a selection of used clothing, books, and home goods. For its designer donations, the Marylebone High Street location is especially well-liked.

The East End Thrift Store is a Whitechapel-based thrift shop that provides a variety of reasonably priced vintage and used clothing as well as sporadic warehouse sales with even bigger discounts.

Camden Market: This enormous market in Camden offers a variety of food and drink vendors as well as a mix of vintage and modern clothing. In the neighborhood, there are also a lot of vintage and used clothing stores.

These are just a few of the fantastic stores in London where you can find vintage and used clothing. It doesn't matter if you're searching for a one-of-a-kind vintage find or a secondhand item at a great price—this city is sure to have something to suit your tastes.

Markets and Street Vendors

London is renowned for its thriving street markets and food carts that provide a wide variety of goods and experiences. Here are some of London's top markets and food stands to visit:

Fresh produce, baked goods, cheese, and charcuterie are just a few of the artisanal and specialty foods available at Borough Market in Southwark. There are also many street food vendors selling everything from French crepes to Indian dosas.

Portobello Road Market: Located in Notting Hill, this well-known market offers a variety of antiques, street food, and vintage clothing and accessories. The market is famous for its Saturday antiques market, which offers a variety of unusual and uncommon finds.

Fresh flowers, plants, and a variety of artisanal food and drink vendors are all available at the vibrant Columbia Road Flower Market in East London. On Sundays, the market is open and very well-liked by both locals and visitors.

Brick Lane Market: Along with its vintage and thrift shops, East London's Brick Lane Market is also home to a number of street food vendors and independent designers who create their own jewelry, clothing, and accessories.

Camden Market: This enormous market in Camden offers a variety of food and drink vendors as well as a mix of vintage and modern clothing. In the neighborhood, there are also a lot of vintage and used clothing stores.

Greenwich Market: This covered market in Greenwich sells a variety of handcrafted items, local specialties, and antiques. The market is open every day and is renowned for its assortment of distinctive and one-of-a-kind goods.

The markets and street vendors in London are countless; these are merely a few examples. Whatever your tastes, you're sure to find something in this energetic city, whether you're looking for fresh produce, artisanal food, vintage finds, or handmade crafts.

London's Fashion History and Trends

London has a long history of fashion and has been instrumental in influencing international trends. Following are some significant fashion milestones and current trends from London:

1960s: In London, the Swinging Sixties saw the emergence of legendary fashion figures like Mary Quant, who popularized the mini skirt, and the Beatles, who popularized Nehru jackets and bell-bottom trousers.

1970s: In the 1970s, punk fashion first appeared in London, thanks in large part to the work of Vivienne Westwood and Malcolm McLaren. Their styles, which included ripped clothing, studded leather, and safety pins, later served as an inspiration for many generations of disobedient fashion enthusiasts.

1980s: Under the direction of designers like Vivienne Westwood and Zandra Rhodes, the New Romantic movement in London during the 1980s saw the emergence of flamboyant, theatrical clothing.

Streetwear also became more popular during this time, with names like Benetton and Adidas becoming more well-known.

1990s: A blend of grunge and minimalist styles dominated the London fashion scene in the 1990s. For their avant-garde designs, designers like John Galliano and Alexander McQueen became well-known worldwide.

Early in the new millennium, new designers like Christopher Kane emerged on the London fashion scene, giving the industry a new, upbeat perspective. Fast fashion also gained popularity during this time period, with names like Topshop and ASOS becoming well-known.

Today: The fashion scene in London is diverse and ever-changing. Emerging designers like Richard Quinn and Grace Wales Bonner are pushing the limits of fashion, while established designers like Burberry and Stella McCartney continue to have a significant impact on the industry.

Streetwear, gender-neutral clothing, and sustainable fashion are some of the current trends in London.

Twice a year, London Fashion Week showcases the best of the local fashion scene and draws visitors from all over the world, including designers, models, and fashion enthusiasts.

CHAPTER 7

OUTDOOR ADVENTURES

Parks and Green Spaces

Beautiful parks and other green areas can be found all over London, providing a tranquil respite from the bustle of the city. Here are a few of London's most well-liked parks and green areas:

Hyde Park is a stunning oasis in the middle of the city and one of London's biggest parks. It has stunning monuments, gardens, and fountains in addition to a lake where guests can rent rowboats.

Regents Park: A sizable park in London, Regents Park is renowned for its beautiful rose gardens and for housing the London Zoo.

Hampstead Heath is a sizable, hilly park in North London that provides breathtaking panoramas of the city. Additionally, it has tennis courts, a running track, and swimming ponds.

Greenwich Park is a lovely park with breathtaking views of the River Thames and the city skyline. It is situated in the southeast of London. The Royal Observatory and the Prime Meridian Line are also located there.

Kew Gardens: Kew Gardens is a must-see location for nature lovers and a UNESCO World Heritage Site. It has lovely gardens, greenhouses, and a walkway above the trees.

Hundreds of deer can be found in Richmond Park, the biggest Royal Park in London, where they are allowed to roam at will. Additionally, it has lovely gardens and walking paths.

East London's Victoria Park is a sizable park with a playground, a bandstand, and a boating lake.

A smaller park in West London, Holland Park is renowned for its stunning Japanese gardens and the old Holland House.

Cycling and Walking Routes

There are numerous cycling and walking routes in London that provide interesting viewpoints of the city, making it a great place to explore on foot or by bicycle. Here are some of London's top walking and cycling routes:

Thames Path: From the River Thames' source in Gloucestershire to the Thames Barrier in London, a 184-mile walking path called the Thames Path follows the river. The Tower Bridge and the Houses of Parliament are two of London's most recognizable landmarks that the path passes through.

Regent's Canal: The 14-mile-long Regent's Canal travels through North London. A well-traveled path for cyclists and pedestrians, the canal's towpath runs through some of London's most energetic communities, including Camden, Hackney, and Limehouse.

Richmond Park: With more than 12 miles of cycling and walking paths, Richmond Park is the largest Royal Park in London. Numerous deer reside in the park, and the paths provide breathtaking views of the park's scenery and wildlife.

The Greenway: The Greenway is an East London-based 4-mile walking and cycling path. The path circles the London Olympic Park and provides views of some of the city's most recognizable modern buildings.

The Jubilee Walkway is a 15-mile walking path that passes by some of London's most well-known sites, such as Buckingham Palace, Trafalgar Square, and Tower Bridge.

Lee Valley Regional Park: From Ware in Hertfordshire to East India Dock Basin in London, the Lee Valley Regional Park is a 26-mile-long park. The park's numerous hiking, biking, and running trails provide breathtaking views of the park's wildlife and other natural splendor.

These routes provide a distinct perspective of the city and a wonderful way to discover some of London's most stunning parks and landmarks.

Kayaking and Boat Tours

Another fantastic way to see London from a different angle is through kayaking and boat tours. Some of London's top kayaking and boat tours are listed below:

A unique way to explore the city is by kayaking on the River Thames. You can go on a variety of kayaking excursions, including ones that take you through the center of the city, past well-known sights like the Tower Bridge, and into the serene canals of East London.

Thames Clippers River Bus: In addition to being a fantastic way to get around the city, the Thames Clippers River Bus is a commuter service. You can take the boats from one end of the city to the other, passing by many well-known landmarks along the way. They are quick and comfortable.

City Cruises: City Cruises provides a variety of boat tours, such as speedboat rides, lunch and dinner cruises, and sightseeing tours. Their boats provide a great way to view the city's landmarks from the water and leave from a number of locations along the Thames.

The Electric Barge: Seeing London on the Electric Barge is a truly unique experience. The Regents Canal offers tours on this fully electric boat that is powered by renewable energy, passing through some of London's most energetic neighborhoods.

The London Kayak Company provides kayaking tours that take you through East London's canals. The knowledgeable guides on the tours provide a distinctive way to see some of London's hidden gems.

Viewing London from the water is an unforgettable experience that will give you a different perspective on the city, whether you decide to kayak or take a boat tour.

Open-Air Markets and Festivals

Throughout the year, there are a lot of outdoor markets and festivals in London that provide a wide selection of cuisine, beverages, music, artwork, and other cultural experiences. Here are some of London's top outdoor markets and festivals:

Borough Market: Located in Southwark, Borough Market is a historic food market that features a wide selection of artisanal foods, street food stalls, and fresh produce. It is open from Monday to Saturday and is a well-liked tourist destination.

Camden Market: Camden Market is a bustling market with a variety of food, fashion, and art stalls that is situated in the center of Camden. It is available every day and a wonderful location to learn about Camden's distinctive culture.

Columbia Road Flower Market: This well-liked Sunday market offers a selection of flowers, plants, and garden supplies. It's a vibrant and lively market that's ideal for a Sunday morning stroll and is situated in the East End.

Notting Hill Carnival: Notting Hill Carnival is an annual street festival that takes place over the long weekend in August to honor the culture and traditions of the Caribbean. The biggest street festival in Europe, it draws tens of thousands of people each year.

Ice skating, Christmas markets, and fairground rides are just a few of the festive pursuits available at the yearly Winter Wonderland festival in Hyde Park. During the holidays, families and friends frequently travel there.

Greenwich Market: Located in Greenwich, Greenwich Market is a historic covered market with a variety of craft, vintage clothing, and food stalls. It is a fantastic location to learn about Greenwich's history and culture and is open every day.

The Southbank Centre Food Market is a weekly outdoor market with a variety of food and drink stalls that is situated on the banks of the Thames. Every Friday, Saturday, and Sunday it is open, and both locals and tourists enjoy going there.

CHAPTER 8

FAMILY-FRIENDLY ACTIVITIES

Museums and Exhibitions for Kids

With so many museums and exhibitions that are both entertaining and educational, London is a great city for kids of all ages. The following are some of London's top children's museums and exhibits:

The Natural History Museum is a well-liked family destination because it offers a variety of interactive exhibits and kid-friendly activities. In a fun and interesting way, children can learn about dinosaurs, animals, and the natural world.

The Science Museum: With a variety of interactive exhibits that explore the world of science and technology, the Science Museum is another well-liked family destination. Children can experience a flight simulator and learn about robots and space.

The V&A Museum of Childhood is a museum with many kid-friendly interactive exhibits and activities that is devoted to the history of childhood. Children can study the history of toys, games, and other elements of childhood.

The London Transport Museum: With many exhibits and activities that explore the history of London's transportation system, the London Transport Museum is a great museum for kids who love transportation. Even bus simulators are accessible to kids.

The Horniman Museum and Gardens is a kid-friendly museum with a variety of exhibits and activities that look at both the natural world and various cultures from around the globe. In the interactive music gallery, kids can learn about animals, plants, and even play music.

The British Museum: The British Museum offers a variety of kid-friendly exhibits and activities, including many interactive displays that examine ancient cultures and civilizations from around the world.

These are just a handful of the many kid-friendly museums and exhibitions in London. With so many options, this vibrant city has something for every child to enjoy and learn from.

Family-Friendly Theater Performances

There are numerous family-friendly theater productions in London that are ideal for children of all ages, but the city is best known for its West End theater district. The following are some of London's top family-friendly theater productions:

The Lion King is a well-known musical that is excellent for families with children of all ages. Astonishing puppetry, vibrant costumes, and upbeat music are used in the production to bring the animals of the African savannah to life on stage.

Matilda: Another well-liked musical that is ideal for families is Matilda. The show, which is based on the beloved Roald Dahl book, tells the tale of a young girl with supernatural abilities who battles her evil school headmistress despite all odds.

A fun and enjoyable musical has been created based on the beloved children's book The Wind in the Willows.

The series follows the exploits of Toad, Ratty, Mole, and Badger as they enjoy themselves while traveling through the countryside.

The Gruffalo is a well-known children's book that has been turned into a stage production that is ideal for young children. The performance includes vibrant sets and costumes, catchy tunes, and a lot of audience participation.

The Railway Children is a heartwarming tale about a family that relocates to the country and makes friends with the neighborhood train station. A real steam train appears on stage during the performance, making it a fantastic choice for families with young children.

These are just a few of London's numerous family-friendly theatrical productions. Everyone can enjoy something and enjoy the magic of live theater in this vibrant city with so many options available.

Fun Parks and Play Areas

For families with children, London has a variety of fun parks and playgrounds. Here are some of London's top parks and playgrounds:

Hyde Park: One of London's biggest parks, Hyde Park offers a range of play areas for kids of all ages. There is a playground, a sizable sandpit, a wading pool, and lots of room to run around and play games in the park.

St. James's Park: In the center of London, there is a lovely park called St. James's Park. There is a sizable playground in the park with a range of playthings, such as swings, slides, and climbing structures. Along with a lot of grassy areas for picnics and games, there is a sandpit, a water play area, and other amenities.

Diana, Princess of Wales Memorial Playground: Situated in Kensington Gardens, this special playground honors Diana, Princess of Wales.

The playground, which takes its design cues from the Peter Pan story, includes a sensory trail, a colossal pirate ship, and a teepee camp.

Coram's Fields: Located in the center of London, Coram's Fields is a special park created with kids in mind. A large adventure playground, a climbing frame, and several other play areas can be found in the park. Children can also interact with animals at a nearby small farm.

Children can learn and play in the Science Museum, which is a wonderful place for them to visit. The museum features several interactive exhibits, such as a hands-on gallery where kids can playfully explore science and technology.

These are just a few of London's many entertaining parks and play areas. With so many options, there is something to enjoy and discover for everyone in this dynamic city.

Animal Encounters and Zoos

There are many fantastic zoos and animal encounters in London that are ideal for families with young children. Some of the top choices are as follows:

One of the oldest and most well-known zoos in the world is ZSL London Zoo. More than 700 different species of animals live in the zoo, including gorillas, lions, tigers, and penguins.

A wide range of interactive exhibits are also available at the zoo, like the Land of the Lions display, where visitors can stroll through a recreation of an Indian village and get up close to the magnificent Asiatic lions.

Families that enjoy sea life should consider visiting SEA LIFE London. More than 600 different species of marine life, including sharks, rays, turtles, and seahorses, call the aquarium home.

Additionally, there are interactive exhibits at the aquarium, like the Ocean Tunnel, which allows visitors to walk through an underwater tunnel while watching sharks and other animals swim above them.

London Wetland Centre: The London Wetland Centre is a distinctive nature preserve where numerous wetland birds and other animals can be found. Visitors can observe various species of wildlife in their natural habitats at the reserve's interactive exhibits, like the Wild Side Walk. Children can also explore play areas and nature trails.

Children under the age of six should consider visiting Battersea Park Children's Zoo. Numerous animals, including farm animals, meerkats, and monkeys, can be found in the zoo. Children can interact with the animals in a petting zoo and various play areas.

Hackney City Farm is a community-run farm where a variety of farm animals, including cows, pigs, and chickens, are kept. Visitors can learn about sustainable farming and gardening techniques in the farm's garden.

CHAPTER 9

DAY TRIPS FROM LONDON

Stonehenge and Salisbury

One of the most recognizable and enigmatic ancient structures in the entire world is Stonehenge. This ancient structure, which is about 90 miles southwest of London, is made up of a circle of standing stones, some of which can weigh up to 25 tons. The monument, which is thought to have been built around 3000 BC, has long been the focus of much discussion and conjecture.

In order to learn more about the site's significance and history, visitors to Stonehenge can either explore it on their own or join a guided tour. A visitor center with interactive exhibits and displays about the monument and its surroundings is also located on the property.

The charming town of Salisbury, which has a stunning cathedral that was built in the 13th century, is only a short drive from Stonehenge. The Salisbury Cathedral is renowned for its 404-foot spire, which is the tallest in the nation. It is one of the best examples of Gothic architecture in England.

Visitor attractions in Salisbury include Old Sarum Hill Fort, an Iron Age fort, as well as the city's historic streets and structures. The Salisbury Museum and the Mompesson House are just two of the many museums in Salisbury that provide insights into the city's rich history and culture.

In conclusion, anyone with an interest in history or archaeology should visit Salisbury and Stonehenge. This region of England is an absolutely unforgettable travel destination because of its gorgeous natural landscape and rich cultural heritage.

Oxford and Cambridge

The most renowned university cities in the world, Oxford and Cambridge, are situated in the south of England. These cities are well-liked among tourists from all over the world because of their beautiful riverside settings, world-class educational institutions, and historic architecture.

One of the oldest and most prestigious universities in the world, the University of Oxford, is located in Oxford. The university's picturesque campus can be explored by guests, and it is full of magnificent structures, courtyards, and gardens. Highlights include the Radcliffe Camera, a striking circular library that is one of Oxford's most recognizable landmarks, and the Bodleian Library, one of the largest and oldest libraries in the world.

Oxford is home to many interesting historical and cultural sites in addition to its academic draws. The city's historic center, which is dotted with antiquated churches, bars, and winding streets, can be explored on foot by visitors.

The Ashmolean Museum, which has a sizable collection of artwork and artifacts, and the Oxford Botanic Garden, the country's first botanical garden, are two other well-liked attractions.

The University of Cambridge, a renowned university that has its roots in the 13th century, is located in Cambridge. Visitors are welcome to tour the university's historic colleges, many of which have served as backdrops for films and television programs. Additional highlights include the Fitzwilliam Museum, which houses a varied collection of art and antiquities, and the Cambridge University Botanic Garden, which has a wide variety of exotic plants and flowers.

Cambridge is a bustling, multicultural city with a rich cultural scene in addition to its academic attractions. At venues like the Cambridge Corn Exchange, visitors can take in performances, concerts, and other cultural events. They can also stroll along the River Cam to see the city's renowned punts and take in the sights of its historic bridges and structures.

Overall, visiting Oxford and Cambridge provides a special window into the country's rich educational and cultural heritage. These cities are a must-visit for anyone interested in history, culture, or education because of their stunning architecture, prestigious universities, and cultural landmarks.

Bath and The Cotswolds

The south-west of England is home to some of the most picturesque locales, including Bath and the Cotswolds. These regions are well-liked travel destinations for tourists from all over the world due to their charming rural landscapes, historic buildings, and rich cultural heritage.

Bath is renowned for its beautifully preserved Roman baths and Georgian architecture and is a **UNESCO World Heritage Site**. Visitors can stroll through the picturesque streets of the city center, which are dotted with historic buildings, shops, and restaurants, or take a tour of the historic Roman Baths, where they can learn about the history and culture of the city.

Other well-liked sights include Bath Abbey, a magnificent example of Gothic architecture, and the Jane Austen Centre, which honors the well-known author who once resided in Bath.

On the other hand, the Cotswolds, an area of exceptional natural beauty, is made up of over 800 square miles of gently rolling hills, quaint villages, and ancient market towns. Visitors can hike along one of the many trails that wind through the area or take a scenic drive through the countryside.

The charming villages of Bibury and Bourton-on-the-Water, the ruins of Hailes Abbey, and the magnificent gardens of Blenheim Palace are just a few of the historical sites and cultural landmarks that can be visited.

In conclusion, a visit to Bath and the Cotswolds presents a special chance to take in some of the best of England's history, culture, and unspoiled landscape. For anyone looking to experience the best that England has to offer, these regions are a must-see because of their charming architecture, breathtaking rural landscapes, and rich cultural heritage.

Brighton and The Seaside

On England's south coast, the quaint seaside community of Brighton can be found. It is a well-liked vacation spot for both tourists and locals due to its fascinating history, vibrant culture, and stunning beachfront. From strolling along the renowned Brighton Pier to discovering the thriving street art scene, visitors to Brighton can engage in a variety of enjoyable activities.

The Royal Pavilion, which was constructed in the 19th century as a seaside retreat for King George IV, is one of Brighton's most well-known attractions. The palace is renowned for both its stunning gardens, which are a favorite place for picnics and relaxation, and its distinctive architecture, which combines elements of Chinese and Indian design.

Another well-liked destination is Brighton's beachfront, where guests can relax in the sun, go swimming in the ocean, and engage in a variety of water sports, such as windsurfing and paddleboarding.

With its amusement park rides, video games, and food vendors, the well-known Brighton Pier is a must-see attraction.

Brighton is renowned for its vibrant cultural scene in addition to its beaches and other attractions. The town is known for its street art scene, which includes works by local and international artists, and is home to a wide variety of art galleries, theaters, and music venues.

Overall, a visit to Brighton is a must for anyone looking to experience the best of England's coast because it provides the ideal fusion of seaside charm, history, and culture.

Brighton is a town where everyone can find something to enjoy thanks to its breathtaking beachfront, distinctive architecture, and vibrant cultural scene.

CHAPTER 10

PLANNING YOUR TRIP

Tips for Budget Travel

Although it can be expensive to travel to London, it is possible to take advantage of everything it has to offer without going over budget. Here are some recommendations for travel in London on a budget:

Utilize public transportation: London has a robust network of overground trains, the tube, and buses. There are numerous ways to save money on transportation, including purchasing a Travelcard or making use of a contactless payment card. Using public transportation is frequently less expensive than using taxis or private vehicles.

Eat at neighborhood markets and food trucks: London has a fantastic street food scene, with a number of neighborhood markets and food trucks providing a wide selection of inexpensive and delectable meals.

For some of the best street food in the city, consider going to Boxpark Shoreditch, Borough Market, or Camden Market.

Look for free attractions: The British Museum, the National Gallery, and the Tate Modern are just a few of the many free museums, galleries, and other attractions in London. For a list of free events and activities, visit websites like Time Out London or Visit London.

Stay in a cheap hotel: Hostels, low-cost hotels, and Airbnb rentals are just a few of the many affordable lodging options in London. Look for lodgings in areas that are further from the city center, like Hackney or Brixton, as they are frequently less expensive than those in more prominent locations.

Walking or cycling are excellent ways to get some exercise while also exploring the city. There are numerous bike paths and bike rental programs available, and many of London's attractions are close to one another.

You can take advantage of everything London has to offer while staying within your budget by using these suggestions. No matter what your budget, you can enjoy London thanks to its rich history, culture, and attractions.

Accommodation Options in London

London offers a variety of lodging choices to fit a variety of needs and preferences. Some of the most well-liked choices are as follows:

London has a wide variety of hotels, from inexpensive to luxurious. Inns from well-known chains like Premier Inn, Travelodge, and Holiday Inn Express provide inexpensive lodging options throughout the city. The Ritz, The Savoy, and The Dorchester are just a few of the upscale accommodations that can be found in central London.

Hostels: For travelers on a tight budget, hostels are a popular choice. In addition to private rooms and dormitory-style rooms, many hostels in London also provide en-suite bathrooms. YHA London St. Pancras, Safestay London Elephant & Castle, and Generator Hostel London are a few of the city's well-known hostels.

Vacation rentals: Apartments, studios, and homes are available all over London through services like Airbnb. Families or groups who prefer more room and the freedom to prepare their own meals may find this option particularly appealing. It's important to remember that vacation rentals are subject to local laws and ordinances, so thorough research is required before making a reservation.

Serviced apartments are a great choice for visitors who will be in London for a longer amount of time. In comparison to a hotel room, they provide more room and amenities, such as a fully functional kitchen, laundry facilities, and frequently a living area. The Ascott Limited, Cheval Residences, and SACO The Serviced Apartment Company are a few well-known serviced apartment providers in London.

Bed and Breakfasts: Bed and breakfasts are a great choice for tourists looking for a more intimate setting. They provide a cozier setting and frequently include a filling breakfast in the rate. The Lilac Door, The Lidos Hotel, and B&B Belgravia are a few well-known bed and breakfasts in London.

Whatever your needs or preferences, there are a variety of accommodations in London that can meet them. To get the best deals and availability, careful research and advanced reservations are essential.

Hotels in London for Travelers

From inexpensive hostels to upscale hotels, London provides a variety of lodging choices for tourists. Here are a few recommendations for lodging in London:

The Hoxton offers stylish rooms with a variety of amenities, including free Wi-Fi, a daily breakfast bag, and an on-site restaurant and bar, all of which are located in the hip Shoreditch neighborhood.

The Zetter Townhouse is a boutique hotel with uniquely designed rooms, a cocktail lounge, and a well-liked restaurant. It is situated in the bustling Clerkenwell neighborhood.

CitizenM London Shoreditch - This budget-friendly hotel provides small, fashionable rooms with cutting-edge amenities, such as an iPad-controlled mood lighting system and a SmartTV.

The Savoy, one of London's most recognizable luxury hotels, offers tasteful rooms and suites with a variety of extras like a spa, 24-hour fitness center, and numerous dining options.

The Nadler Soho offers tastefully decorated rooms with a variety of amenities, including a mini-kitchenette and free Wi-Fi, in the center of London's Soho neighborhood.

In the Dorchester - The Dorchester, another venerable luxury hotel, offers opulent rooms and suites with luxuries like marble bathrooms, round-the-clock room service, and numerous restaurants and bars.

The COMO Halkin - The Halkin, which is situated in the upscale Belgravia district, offers modern rooms and suites with opulent extras like a Michelin-starred restaurant and a private garden.

These are merely a few of the numerous hotels that are offered in London. Finding the best option for your needs and preferences usually requires some research and reading reviews.

Transportation Options in London

Despite the fact that London is a busy city, there are a lot of transportation options available to help you get around. Here are a few of the most well-known:

London Underground (the Tube): With 11 lines connecting more than 270 stations, the Tube is the quickest and most practical way to travel throughout London.

Buses: There are more than 8,000 buses operating on more than 700 routes in London, and they are a great way to see the city.

Taxis: London's well-known black cabs are a recognizable symbol of the city and a practical and dependable mode of transportation.

Uber and other ride-sharing services are also available in London, and they are frequently less expensive than standard taxis.

Bike rental: Santander Cycles, a bike-sharing program in London, lets you rent a bike for as little as £2.

London is an extremely walkable city, and many of the major attractions are close to one another.

River Thames: With a variety of boat tours and river buses available, the River Thames also offers a distinctive and beautiful way to see the city.

Having an Oyster card or contactless payment card will save you money on fares and make traveling easier when you use public transportation.

Best Times to Visit London

London is a wonderful place to travel all year round because it has something to offer in every season. There are, however, some seasons of the year that are particularly well-liked and provide distinctive experiences. The following suggestions for the ideal times to visit London are provided:

Spring (March–May): Flowers bloom in the parks and gardens, and the weather is usually mild, making London a lovely place to visit. If you want to visit without the summertime crowds, this is a great time to do so.

Summer (June–August): With long days, pleasant weather, and a variety of outdoor festivals and events, summer is London's busiest travel season. However, it can also be very crowded and lodging and attractions can be very expensive.

Autumn (September to November): With the leaves changing color and a variety of fall festivals and events happening, autumn is a lovely time to visit

London. There are fewer people than in the summer and the weather is typically mild.

Winter (December–February): Christmas lights and decorations are everywhere in London during the winter, along with ice skating rinks and holiday markets. However, it can get chilly and rainy, and some attractions might only be open for a shorter period of time.

When making travel plans, it's important to keep in mind that prices for lodging and attractions may be higher during school breaks. Easter (typically in April), summer (July-August), and Christmas (late December to early January) are the main school break times in the UK.

Printed in Great Britain
by Amazon